Resume Writing for Beginners

Learn How to Write a Professional, Winning Resume to Impress the Hiring Manager and Land the Job Interview, and Eventually, the Job You are After

By Clark Darsey

© **Copyright 2020 - All rights reserved.**

The content contained within this book may not be reproduced, duplicated or transmitted without direct written permission from the author or the publisher.

Under no circumstances will any blame or legal responsibility be held against the publisher or author for any damages, reparation, or monetary loss due to the information contained within this book. Either directly or indirectly.

Legal Notice:

This book is copyright protected. This book is only for personal use. You cannot amend, distribute, sell, use, quote or paraphrase any part, or the content within this book, without the consent of the author or publisher.

Disclaimer Notice:

Please note the information contained within this document is for educational and entertainment purposes only. All effort has been executed to present accurate, up to date and reliable, complete information. No warranties of any kind are declared or implied. Readers acknowledge that the author is not engaging in the rendering of legal, financial, medical or professional advice. The content within this book has been derived from various sources. Please consult a licensed professional before attempting any techniques outlined in this book.

By reading this document, the reader agrees that under no circumstances is the author responsible for any losses, direct or indirect, which are incurred as a result of the use of information contained within this document, including, but not limited to, —errors, omissions, or inaccuracies.

Contents

Introduction 1

Chapter 1 - What is a Resume 4

Chapter 2 - Things to Bear In Mind 11

Chapter 3 - Parts of the Resume 19

    The Heading 20

    The Objective Statement 23

    About you: 25

    About the Company or Organization: 26

    Job Experience 30

    Education 34

    Abilities and Qualifications 39

Chapter 4 -- References 46

Chapter 5 - The Cover Letter 50

Chapter 6 - Ensuring You're Ready 57

Chapter 7 - Sample Cover Letters 61

Chapter 8 - Sample Reference Sheets 79

Chapter 9 - The Interview 85

Conclusion 88

Thank you for buying this book and I hope that you will find it useful. If you will want to share your thoughts on this book, you can do so by leaving a review on the Amazon page, it helps me out a lot.

Introduction

Everybody in the business world understands that having a great resume can be the distinction between getting a job and not getting a job. You are going to want to have a resume that is crafted professionally, which is going to reflect you, your job capabilities, and your experience.

Having an excellent looking resume is so crucial when you are looking for a job that it ought to be your top priority. There are all sorts of methods you can use when crafting a resume that works; however, there is no magic formula for a resume that is going to work all the time.

The choice truly is up to you how you create a resume. However, there are specific subtleties that are going to have to be a part of your resume and that every company searches for.

It is simple to create a resume that works; however, it is necessary that you do not ignore what makes your resume most effective. This one or two-page file speaks about you, your capabilities, your experience, your education, and your achievements.

It is the first thing that a possible employer is going to see before he or she meets you, so you want it to truly be engaging and make them wish to get the phone and call you for an interview!

There are all sorts of schools of thought concerning how a resume ought to look, what information it ought to consist of, and how to put it together. Nevertheless, many business folks concur that when they take a look at the resume of a possible employee, they want the resume to be succinct, to the point, and simple to read.

Whichever school of thought you, as a job applicant, subscribe to, you are going to want your resume to be what a possible employer wishes to see. That is why you are going to want as much information about resumes as possible so you can have something that you could be happy to send out as an introduction to you and what you can do for a company.

What I am going to do inside the pages of this book is show you a couple of various methods to craft a resume. We are going to cover the vital parts of this document and show you methods to make your resume a work of art! I am going to additionally provide you with some suggestions and techniques to get your resume noticed over another candidate.

While we're at it, I'll additionally offer you some suggestions about the job interview and what you can do to land that job. Discovering the job of your dreams isn't often as easy as simply completing a job application and, after that, waiting for a call. It takes some proactivity on your part and the right tools. I believe I can assist with that!

Chapter 1 - What is a Resume

A resume is a selling tool that details your abilities and experiences so an employer can see how you can add to the employer's workplace. Your resume needs to sell you in short order.

While you might have all the requirements for a specific position, your resume is a failure if the employer does not quickly come to the conclusion that you "have what it takes."

The most effective resumes are plainly concentrated on a particular job title and deal with the employer's stated requirements for the position. The more you understand about the responsibilities and abilities needed for the job-- and arrange your resume around these points-- the more effective the resume.

You are going to require the information to compose a great resume. Not just information about jobs you have actually held in the past, yet additionally the information to pick the most pertinent achievements, abilities, and experience for THIS position. The more you learn about the employer and the position, the more you can customize your resume to fit the job.

Some individuals think about a resume as their "life on a page," however, how could anybody put everything essential about themselves on a single piece of paper (or two)? Really, resumes are a lot more particular, consisting of just appropriate information about you for particular employers.

Like a life, nevertheless, a resume is constantly growing and altering. As your career goals shift or the job market changes-- as you grow personally and expertly-- odds are you are going to have to re-write your resume or at least produce brand-new versions. Composing a resume is a lifelong procedure.

How do you know what in your life-- past, present, and future-- is most appropriate to potential employers? How do you choose which information to incorporate? The quick answer to both these questions is "it depends." It depends upon your private career goals along with the professional objectives of the companies hiring in your location or field of interest.

In the end, just you, through research, preparation, questioning, and self-reflection, can figure out the shape and content of your resume. However, the methods beneath can assist you in asking the appropriate questions and start exploring your choices.

Depending upon whom you ask, a resume might be considered as the single most important vehicle to getting your next job, or it might be deemed an unneeded annoyance.

In both cases, this is incorrect. A resume is a professional introduction meant to result in a one-on-one interview - the chance for communication that can result in a job offer.

It is an unusual prospect who is employed by his/her resume alone. It is just as uncommon to be offered an interview without one.

A resume is frequently the very first line of contact. It sets up the first impression of a possible job candidate's abilities, background and hiring worth. If composed well, this impression could be a favorable one, providing the reader with a sense of the candidate's "fit" for the position and company being targeted.

If composed truly well, it might encourage the reader that the job candidate is preferably matched for the job. When paired with an effective cover letter, the resume could be a really strong marketing tool.

Preparing a resume might be viewed as an annoyance, however having a sound, properly designed resume is a fundamental part of your job search. Understand that for each available job opening there might be as many as 100 to 1000 resumes sent.

If your resume falls short to properly communicate your hiring worth (for the particular position), falls short of establishing your hiring worth over contending candidates, or is tough to follow, your capability to contend versus those 100 to 1000 professionals vying for the very same position are going to be considerably reduced.

If your resume leads to an interview, it has actually done its job. If it sets you ahead of the competitors in the mind of your interviewer, then it has actually provided you with a distinct benefit and has actually surpassed its job.

A fantastic resume does what all excellent marketing pieces do: it offers the "customer" the "product" (you). Like it or not, the job of trying to find employment is a job in sales and marketing.

The product you are "offering" is you, and the "consumer," who has distinct requirements and interests, has to be sold on the reality that you have what it takes to finish the job and to meet the requirements of the position.

He or she is going to wish to know how you are going to fix his/her issues, and he or she is going to give your resume about 15 seconds or less. 15 seconds is the typical time a hiring manager is going to set aside for a brand-new resume - prior to giving it a prospective "yes" or "no" response.

The resume is not going to get you the job. However, it can definitely boost your odds of being seen and interviewed, just as it can trigger you to be passed over in favor of a candidate who offers a better presentation.

Similar to any kind of marketing campaign, utilize your resume as one tool in your search. Continue to network, enhance your interviewing abilities, and utilize every opportunity offered to you to better your odds and opportunities. And, after you have actually secured that next position, do this all over once again. Constantly be ready for the next chance. Keep your resume up-to-date and remain career fit.

So, basically, a resume is you in short form on paper. That is why having a great-looking, simple to read resume is so essential. Let's take a look at a couple of ideas about your resume from the experts.

Chapter 2 - Things to Bear In Mind

In preparing your resume, the more you learn about the position you are targeting, the better. If you understand the company's objectives and goals, if you comprehend the requirements of the position, if you acknowledge the company's "issues," and if you know who makes up the company's competition, you are going to be prepared.

AND you (and your distinct abilities and experience) can meet the requirements of all the above (you have actually properly evaluated your own worth to those who have actually employed you in the past), you are going to have the material required to produce a successful marketing piece.

As in any kind of marketing material, it is essential to provide the information so that it catches your consumer's interest rapidly. Your objective is to motivate the reader to remain with your document as long as possible. Your odds for a more comprehensive reading boosts when you provide the reader with the information which he or she wishes to see early in the document.

Among the very best methods to achieve this is to develop a Summary Section at the start of your resume. A Summary Area highlights for your reader those personal and professional abilities you have that permit you to excel in your selected field and position.

Items and abilities of greatest importance (from your readers' perspective) ought to be noted in priority, supporting an impression of both "fit" and possible success. In addition, these ought to be elements of your background that set you apart from your contending candidates, especially candidates with skill sets comparable to your own. You are, in effect, revealing your reader how you are going to fix their issues - much better than the competitors - and why interviewing you is going to be a beneficial expense of their time.

You are not composing your resume in order to put your career autobiography out there for posterity. This is not about you - seriously. It is about how you can satisfy the requirements of your reader - in this specific position at this specific company. It is everything about them.

Throughout the interview is when your initial chance for negotiation happens and you get to discuss what you get out of the offer. However, right now, the only individual who matters is your reader. They hold all the marbles.

When composing your resume, bear in mind your particular reader. Noting information that is going to be of no worth to the position or company being targeted is simply a waste of time.

Look for redundancy in your declarations. If the positions you have actually held are comparable, then repeating the exact same functions in detail throughout your document is unneeded (heard it, got it). Nevertheless, do not short-change yourself on your achievements.

Your possible employer is most interested in seeing how employing you is going to benefit him/her and the company. If you are handling a hiring manager or human resource director, you can wager he or she has a lot resting on the truth that, if you are employed, they discovered the best individual for the job.

It is pricey to hire, train, and let somebody go - and it is their job to ensure this does not occur. All parties included wish to know they are making the ideal decision, and it is your job to guarantee to them that they are.

The most helpful method to do this is by recognizing how you have actually benefited employers in the past. Take credit for your involvement and achievements. While taking a look at the elements of your background might appear small or of little worth to you, they might be viewed as an important asset to those seeking to fill a requirement.

The design of your resume is essential. Your resume needs to maintain a "tidy" and professional look (keep in mind, it is representing you!). It ought to enable the reader to access the information rapidly. Cool margins, sufficient "white space" in between groupings, and indenting to highlight text, help the ease of reference and retention of the material.

Utilize "bolding" and italics moderately. Overuse of these functions really lessens their effectiveness of promoting the material they are meant to highlight. Your contact information (how the reader can reach you) is basically the most crucial information in the whole file. Make sure your name, address, contact number, and e-mail address (if included) are plainly noticeable and at the top of your file (from habit, this is where your reader is going to try to find this information - do not make them look for it).

If you are incorporating extra pages, be sure that your name is on these secondary pages. Think about including your contact number here, too, in case your sheets end up being separated.

The requirements for resume length have actually altered. It used to be normal for resumes to be one-page in length, and no longer. For prospects with years of experience, having actually held numerous positions, or with impressive accomplishments, this one-page restriction frequently leads to a file that is unreadable, looks "compressed," or makes use of a font style size so little that the reader is needed to squint (no, they will not in fact bother). The one-page standard no longer applies.

Utilize as much space as you require to concisely, precisely, and successfully convey your abilities, history, accomplishments, and achievements - as these relate to the position and business being targeted.

A two-page file, if presented well, is not going to lessen the effectiveness of your marketing approach - as long as the information you offer is relevant and important to your reader's objectives and interests.

A three-page resume is needing much of your reader's time (and patience), and might not be as helpful as a more concise presentation. In scholastic fields and European markets, it might be essential to go over 2 pages in length, however just supply this much information if you definitely can not present your history and accomplishments in less.

If you are certain your reader is going to agree with you, they are not going to mind reading a resume over 3 pages. An excessively long presentation might leave your reader questioning if you could be succinct in anything you do.

Document in detail your latest 10-15 years of work and/or experience. Longer if the most recent position was longer than ten years. Be certain to document the growth in a business where several positions have actually been held, consisting of identification of promotions and increased duties.

List positions held before this in reducing detail, unless a previous position more successfully documents pertinent abilities for the position you are presently targeting.

You wish to attract your reader into wishing to meet you (the interview) to get more information. Existing history and just recently used abilities are going to hold the most worth. Keep in mind, you are going to have a chance to expand on the information in your resume throughout the interview. So, entice your reader to wish to discover more. However, do not forget to leave something to tell.

How do you create a resume that is going to get attention? Let's have a look at each area one by one.

Chapter 3 - Parts of the Resume

Before you compose, make an effort to do a self-assessment on paper. Describe your skills and abilities in addition to your work experience and after-school activities. This is going to make it much easier to prepare an extensive resume.

When you do this, make certain to document dates as it could be essential-- specifically in showing that you have a consistent work history. Spaces in work history do not bear well with possible employers as it gives the impression that you are not reliable.

Gather together the names of businesses you have actually worked for together with their address and contact number and the name of your immediate administrator at the time. Do not include salary history on a basic resume. If salary comes up, it is going to be throughout the interview or at the time you are-- ideally-- offered the job.

Keep in mind the unique accomplishments and awards you have actually gotten in addition to the date you got them. You might additionally wish to include a blurb about the qualifications that had to be met in order to get that award.

However we are getting ahead of ourselves. Let's start with the heading of the resume.

The Heading

The heading of your resume offers standard contact information about you. That indicates your name, address, any contact numbers, and your e-mail address. You can organize this information in a range of ways. The easy way is like this:

Sarah Smith

333 My Bright Way

Yourtown, IL 12345

Home Phone: (222) 222-2222

Mobile Phone: (333) 333-3333

e-mail: ssmith@gmail.com

As you can see, the name remains in bigger print than the remainder of the information and in bold. The remainder of the contact information remains in tinier print and not bolded.

Another format you can utilize for the heading appears like this:

Sarah Smith

333 My Bright Way * Yourtown, IL 12345 * Home Phone (

222) 222-2222 * Cell Phone: (333) 333-3333 * ssmith@gmail.com

Yet another manner in which you can build the heading is like this:

Sarah Smith

333 My Bright Way.

Yourtown, IL 12345.

Home Phone (222) 222-2222 * Mobile Phone (333) 333-3333 * ssmith@gmail.com

The crucial thing to bear in mind about the heading is that it includes your current important information and highlights your name. Here are some other tips to bear in mind when composing the heading of your resume:

- Stay away from nicknames.
- Utilize a permanent address. Utilize your mom's and dad's address, a buddy's address, or the address you intend to utilize after graduation.
- Utilize a long-term phone number and include the area code. If you have a voice mail, record a neutral greeting.
- Include your e-mail address. Lots of employers are going to discover it beneficial. (Note: Pick an e-mail address that sounds professional.).

- Include your website address just if the websites reflects your professional aspirations.

The next part is your objective statement.

The Objective Statement

There are 2 schools of thought relating to an objective statement. Some individuals claim you should not include this on a resume since that is what your cover letter is for. Other individuals claim that mentioning what you wish to achieve in your career is most likely the most fundamental part of the resume.

You can select to add an objective statement if you like, however, if you do, you want to understand a couple of things. Most importantly, this statement ought to be quick and succinct-- not more than a sentence or 2. An objective informs prospective employers of the sort of work you intend to do.

Specify the job you want. For instance: To acquire an entry-level position within a financial institution needing strong analytical and organizational abilities. Tailor your objective to each employer you target/every job you look for.

Objective statements enhance your resume by assisting you to:

- Highlight your primary certifications and summarize them for readers.

- Notify your readers of the position(s) you are looking for and your career goals.

- Develop your professional identity.

To enhance your odds for success, it's constantly a great idea to customize your objective statement (along with your entire resume and cover letter) to specific companies and/or positions. This indicates, for instance, calling a position by the name the company utilizes to explain it. You may even suggest the organization's name in your statement.

Make every effort to match your certifications with those preferred by the company. If you are not sure what your résumé's readers are going to be searching for, you'll want to do some research to offer your objective statement a competitive edge.

Prior to preparing or revising your objective statement, you are going to find it useful to respond to as many of the following questions as possible.

About you:

- What are your primary qualifications (strengths, abilities, areas of expertise)?
- What positions (or a variety of positions) do you look for?
- What are your professional goals?
- What kind of company or work setting are you interested in?

About the Company or Organization:

- Which of your qualifications are most wanted by your résumé's readers?
- What position titles (or range or positions) are offered?
- What are some objectives of the organizations that intrigue you?
- What kinds of organizations or work settings are now hiring?

The most typical error made in writing objective claims is being too general and unclear in explaining either the position wanted or your qualifications.

For instance, some objective statements are like this:

An internship enabling me to utilize my knowledge and proficiency in various areas.

Such an objective statement raises more questions than it addresses: What type of internship? What knowledge? What type of proficiency? Which areas?

Be as specific as possible in your objective statement to assist your readers in seeing what you can offer "at a glimpse."

To come up with an objective statement that works, have a go at one of these formulas:

1. To stress a specific position and your relevant qualifications.

A position as a [name or kind of position] enabling me to utilize my [qualifications]

To use my [qualifications] as a [position title]

A position as a Support Specialist permitting me to utilize my abilities in the fields of computer science and management information systems

2. To stress the field or kind of organization you wish to work in and your professional objective or your primary qualifications

A chance to [professional objective] in a [kind of organization, work environment, or field]

To go into [kind of organization, work environment, or field] enabling me to utilize my [qualifications]

A chance to acquire a loan officer position, with ultimate advancement to the vice president for lending services, in a growth-oriented bank.

To sign up with an aircraft research group enabling me to use my understanding of avionics and aircraft electrical systems.

3. To highlight your professional goal or an organizational objective

To [professional goal]

A chance to [professional objective]

To assist kids and households in struggling circumstances by using my child protection services background

4. A particular position wanted

[position name]

A technical writer specializing in the user documentation

Some things to remember when developing your objective statement consist of the following:

- Incorporate keywords and phrases utilized in the job ad(s).
- Have fun with word choices to fit your strengths and your readers' expectations. You may try.

o substituting for "utilize" words such as "develop," "apply," or "employ," and so on

o changing "enabling me" with "requiring" or "offering me the chance," and so on

o changing "go into" to "join," "pursue," "acquire," "become a member," "contribute," and so on

Mix 2 or more of the models above or produce your own!

Depending upon the format of your resume, the objective part ought to be written in sentence format with its own heading.

The next 2 parts are interchangeable depending upon which applies the most to the position you are applying for. If you believe your job experience is more pertinent to the job, then list "job experience" next. If it is your education that is going to assist you the most, then put that part next.

Job Experience.

This is the most complicated part of your resume, and it is needed, although you have a lot of flexibility in the way you demonstrate your experiences. To begin with this part, make a list of your job titles and the names, dates, and places of locations where you worked.

Break each job (paid or unpaid) into brief, detailed phrases or sentences that start with action verbs. These phrases are going to highlight the abilities you utilized on the job and assist the employer in seeing you as a go-getter in the work environment. Utilize action words to illustrate the work you did.

You might select special typestyles, bolding, highlighting, or placement to draw your reader's attention to the information you wish to highlight. When the company you worked for is more remarkable than your job title, you might wish to highlight that information.

Quickly offer the employer a summary of work that has actually taught you abilities. Include your work experience in reverse chronological order-- that is, put your last job initially and work backward to your initial, relevant job. Include:

- Title of position,
- Name of the company
- Location of work (town, state).
- Dates of work.

- Explain your work obligations with a focus on particular abilities and accomplishments.

You should most likely not go back more than your 3 previous jobs so that your resume does not get too long. Nevertheless, you are going to wish to include any job experience that pertains to the job you are making an application for to demonstrate you have experience in that field.

Depending upon how you are formatting your resume, there are a number of manners in which you can put this part together. Here are a number of ways in which you can have a go at this:

April, 2011 – Present

ABC Corporation; Anywhere, IL.

Position: Sales Analyst.

Responsibilities: To keep track of sales activities for 20 salespeople, compute profit/loss margins, make recommendations for improvement, hold instructional workshops to guarantees sales are progressing as they should, prepare yearly statements, create and execute brand-new procedures to enhance efficiency.

ABC Corporation; Anywhere, IL.

April, 2011 - Present.

Position: Sales Analyst.

Tasks: To keep an eye on sales activities for 20 salespeople, compute, profit/loss margins, make recommendations for enhancement, hold instructional workshops to guarantee sales is advancing as it should, prepare yearly statements, create and execute brand-new procedures to enhance efficiency.

ABC Corporation; Anywhere, IL.

April, 2011 - Present.

Sales Analyst.

- To keep an eye on sales activities for 20 salespeople.
- Compute, profit/loss margins.
- Make recommendations for enhancement.

- Hold instructional workshops to make sure sales are progressing as they should.
- Prepare yearly statements.
- Create and execute brand-new procedures to enhance efficiency.

There are many, many more manners in which you can design this part, and everything depends upon how your whole resume is set out. As long as you have the fundamental information about what organization you worked for, when you worked for them, your position at the company, and your job responsibilities, then you ought to be covered.

Next is the education part.

Education

This part could be established just like the job experience part-- all of it truly depends upon what format you are selecting for your resume. This part is an essential one for the majority of students, and it is a required component of the resume. In this part, you ought to include:

- The name and location of your college or university
- Your degree and graduation date
- Your major(s) and minor(s).
- Grade point average.

Utilize placement of information, bold type or underlining to emphasize the features you wish to highlight. It is often required to identify a feature or features that make you stand apart among other students.

For instance, students bold their university or college in case they feel like that is a distinguishing characteristic. Others might choose to bold their kind of degree. New graduates without a great deal of work experience ought to note their educational information initially. Alumni can note it after the work experience part.

Make certain the following is featured in the education part of your resume:

- Your newest educational information is noted initially.
- Include your degree (A.S., B.S., B.A., and so on).
- Your major, institution attended, and your minor/concentration.
- Include your grade point average (GPA) in case it is higher than 3.0.
- Reference academic honors.

Here are 2 instances of education parts, with various information highlighted.

Purdue University, West Lafayette, Indiana.

Bachelor of Science, May 2010.

Major: Supervision; GPA 5.5/ 6.0.

Bachelor of Science in Accounting, May 2011.

Minor in Finance, GPA: 5.5/ 6.0 Major, 5.2/ 6.0 Overall.

Purdue University, West Lafayette, Indiana.

In your education part, you might wish to feature a number of sub-groups-- particularly in case you are a current graduate trying to find your initial position. The very first sub-group is "Related Course Work."

This is an optional part of your Education part, which could be rather remarkable and informative for prospective employers. Students looking for internships might wish to note all finished major-related courses.

Graduates may note job-related courses different than those needed to get the degree (employers are going to already be aware of those). Include top-level courses in optional concentrations, foreign languages, computer applications, or communications classes. You might select more significant headings like "Computer Applications" if you want to highlight specific parts.

Keep in mind - employers and recruiters are familiar with the fundamental courses needed in your major. Restrict these parts to special courses or abilities you have to offer.

Another optional sub-group in the education part is "Special Projects." This optional part might be included to point out special features of your education that are especially fascinating to employers or that might make you more competent than others for the job you are looking for.

Students typically include research, writing, or computer projects. Restrict your description to the essential truths. You might broaden your discussion in your application letter.

If you like, you can include any awards you got or special accomplishments in this part, however, the majority of resumes are going to have a different part for this to cover not just academic awards yet additionally business awards.

Our next part pertains to your special capabilities as they apply to the position you are attempting to land.

Abilities and Qualifications

While not all resumes consist of an abilities part, this might be valuable when you wish to highlight the abilities you have actually gotten from your numerous jobs or activities, rather than the responsibilities, or the job title.

If you do not have ample previous experience for a particular job you are looking for, it is essential to stress your abilities relating to that job.

Abilities can be just as crucial as work experience to employers. To prepare this part, you ought to:

- List jobs, activities, projects, and special offices.
- Think about the abilities you have actually acquired through those experiences.
- Group these abilities into 3 - 5 job-related abilities categories and utilize these as headings.
- Note your abilities with substantial details under the headings.

- Organize headings in order of importance as they relate to your career goal.
- Organize abilities under headings in order of importance according to your objective.

In this part, you are going to additionally wish to include any workplace machines you have experience operating, software programs you have actually ended up being competent in, and anything else that you feel may put you over the top with the job.

Example:

Leadership

- I carried out regular monthly club and board meetings for Lafayette Junior Woman's Club.
- I Headed club's $9,000 philanthropic project sponsored by Tippecanoe County Historical Association.
- I Coordinated the duties of committees to offer and serve food to 1000 individuals at a fundraising event.

Business Communication

- I finished a formal report for the Business Writing course.
- I composed yearly state and district reports of all club's community service projects, volunteered hours, and financial contributions.
-

Financial Management

- I monitored the collection and dispersion of $5,000 in funds to different agencies and projects.

- I composed and examined regular business statements concerning funds to particular projects/agencies.

The next part could be worded in a number of various ways. Here is where you wish to let the possible employer understand you have actually taken part in activities and events, along with the fact that you belong to professional organizations together with any special awards that you have actually gotten.

A great deal of this depends upon whether you are fresh out of school trying to find your very first job or if you have actually been in the business world and are making an application for another job.

Awards and Accomplishments

You can pick a couple of various methods to word this part. If you like, it could be entitled "Activities and Honors" or "Awards and Organizations." It actually depends on you. You need to customize your resume to your particular requirements.

This optional part mentions your leadership, sociability and energy level as revealed by your participation in various activities. This ought to be your shortest part and ought to support your career goals. Extra information about activities could be included in your application letter or gone over in your interview.

You ought to:

- Select just activities and honors that support your career goal.
- Note your college or professional organizations and organize them in order of importance as they pertain to your career goal.
- Include any office or official position you held.
- Point out any acronyms your employer might not understand.
- Include dates.

Example:

Finance Club, President

Gamma Professional Fraternity

Purdue Grand Prix Foundation, President

Purdue Association for the Education of Young Children (PAEYC).

For any awards, you ought to feature the year you got the award. You additionally might wish to include a short breakdown of the criteria that you needed to meet in order to get that honor.

Lastly, you are going to conclude your resume with a reference part.

References

This is the smallest part of your resume due to the fact that it ought to just include one sentence-- "References are available upon request." You typically should not incorporate references on your resume. You are going to put your references on a different reference sheet which we are going to deal with in the next part.

If the job you are making an application for asks in the ad to incorporate references when you send in your resume, you ought to change the "References" part to read "References are attached."

Chapter 4-- References.

You are going to wish to have numerous individuals on hand who are going to vouch for you as far as your character, your work habits, your work principles, and your basic value and worth as an employee and individual.

You are going to wish to have a minimum of 3 references and no more than 5. At least one of these references ought to be an individual reference who is not a relative. It could be a buddy, a colleague, or an acquaintance. The others ought to be work or school references.

The first guideline for references is to ask the person initially if you can utilize them as a reference when making an application for jobs. As long as you have an excellent relationship with them, many people are more than happy to vouch for you and provide you a glowing recommendation.

The function of a reference sheet is to have a list of individuals who can validate and elaborate on your professional experience for a possible employer. Previous employers, professors, and advisors are the very best professional references to have.

It is necessary to have a reference sheet since prospective employers are going to frequently request a list of references they can get in touch with. If you included a statement like "References Available upon Demand" on your resume, you ought to have the ability to produce a reference sheet as quickly as one is asked for. In any case, having a reference sheet is going to spare you time in the future throughout the interview procedure.

Ensure to include individuals who understand what kind of individual you are and who are familiar with your work. It is essential to choose people who understand your distinctiveness so that they can supply a favorable and precise description of you to the employer or company in which you are looking for work.

You must ALWAYS call your references prior to including them on a reference sheet. It is additionally a great idea to provide a copy of your resume and talk with them about the job you are looking for, so they are going to understand how to represent you ideally.

When you are noting your references, you ought to include the following information:

- Your name
- Your present and permanent address(es).
- Your reference person or persons' information that includes that individual's:

o Name.

o Department/Company.

o Title/Position.

o Address.

o Phone number.

o A quick statement regarding how you know this person.

It is not needed to include the tail end-- the statement regarding how you know this person, however, it can assist. That way, if a possible employer does inspect your references, they understand why you wished to note them on your reference sheet.

Another really vital part of the job application procedure is the cover letter that you are going to feature with your resume.

Chapter 5 - The Cover Letter

The function of a cover letter is to present you and your resume, in addition to offering some extra information about yourself to possible employers. You might additionally wish to explain some parts of your resume you want the employer to pay special attention to.

A separately typed cover letter normally accompanies each resume you send out. Your cover letter might make the distinction between acquiring a job interview and having your resume ignored. It makes good sense to dedicate the needed effort and time to compose effective cover letters.

A cover letter ought to complement, not replicate your resume. Its function is to translate the data-oriented, accurate resume and include a personal touch. A cover letter is typically your earliest composed contact with a possible employer, creating a crucial first impression.

There are 3 various types of cover letters:

- The application letter responds to a particular job opening you have seen
- The prospecting letter asks about any job openings
- The networking letter which requests information and helps with your job search

If you are sending a resume, your application cover letter ought to constantly include a line in your cover letter that states where you discovered the ad for the job you are making an application for. You ought to constantly customize your cover letter to the particular job you are making an application for.

It's definitely much easier to compose generic or blanket cover letters than it is to compose a cover letter particularly targeted to each position you make an application for. Nevertheless, if you do not invest the time in composing cover letters, you're most likely not going to get the interview, despite your qualifications.

My initial suggestion in composing a cover letter that works is to make a match between your certifications/education and the job. This takes a while, and it's not easy, however, it is necessary. Take the job posting and list the requirements the employer is trying to find.

Then list the abilities and experience you have. Either address how your abilities match the job in paragraph type or list the requirements and your qualifications. Do not create a kind letter and send it to every prospective employer.

Effective cover letters describe the reasons for your interest in the particular company and determine your most pertinent abilities or experiences (keep in mind, relevance is determined by the company's self-interest). They ought to show a high level of interest and understanding about the position.

To be effective, your cover letter ought to follow the standard format of a common business letter and ought to address 3 standard concerns:

1. First Paragraph - Why you are composing

2. Middle Paragraphs - What you can offer

3. Concluding Paragraph - How you are going to follow-up

In many cases, you might have been referred to a prospective employer by a buddy or associate. Make certain to discuss this mutual contact, by name, in advance because it is most likely to motivate your reader to keep reading!

If you are writing in response to a job posting, note where you learned of the position and the title of the position. More significantly, show your enthusiasm and the likely match in between your qualifications and the position's requirements.

If you are composing a prospecting letter in which you ask about possible job openings - state your particular job goal. Considering that this kind of letter is unsolicited, it is much more essential to catch the reader's attention.

If you are composing a networking letter to approach a person for information, make your demand clear. The benefit of composing a letter like this and including your resume is that you are going to be making contacts in the business world, and when a job opening shows up, they might still have your resume on file. It never ever hurts to be pro-active when trying to find a job!

When replying to an ad, refer particularly to the qualifications noted and highlight how your specific capabilities and experiences connect to the position for which you are applying. In a prospecting letter reveal your capacity to fulfill the employer's requirements instead of concentrating on what the company can provide you.

You can do this by giving evidence that you have actually looked into the company completely and that you possess abilities utilized within that company.

Stress your accomplishments and analytical abilities. Demonstrate how your education and work abilities are transferable, and therefore appropriate, to the position for which you are applying.

End by restating your interest in the job and letting the company understand how they can reach you and include your contact number and/or e-mail address. If you desire, you can try straight for the job interview or informative interview and show that you are going to follow-up with a phone conversation to establish an appointment at an equally convenient time. Make sure to make the call within the time span indicated.

In some circumstances, a company might clearly restrict phone calls or you might be replying to a "blind want-ad," which precludes you from this follow-up. Unless this holds true, make your best shot to reach the organization. At the minimum, you ought to validate that your materials were received and that your application is complete.

If you are applying from outside the employer's geographical location, you might wish to show if you'll remain in town throughout a particular timespan (this makes it simpler for the company to agree to meet with you).

In conclusion, you might show that your references are available on demand. Likewise, if you have a portfolio or composing samples to support your credentials, mention their availability.

So, we have actually covered the 3 crucial files you require in a job search: the resume, the cover letter, and the reference sheet. Before you get thrilled and begin mailing out your creations, there are some things that you want to do before that.

Chapter 6 - Ensuring You're Ready

You are attempting to get a job, and you are all prepared with your resume, reference sheet, and cover letter. Before you get all thrilled and put your info in the mail, you are going to wish to go through a couple of checkpoints.

Primarily, run a spell check on your computer. However, do not stop there. Read your files over and over to ensure there are no typographical or grammatical mistakes. It may additionally assist to have another person read over them also to be sure that it looks the way it should.

The more individuals who see your resume, the most likely that misspelled words and uncomfortable phrases are going to be seen (and fixed).

Here is a list to bear in mind for your cover letter:

- The contact name and business name are accurate
- The letter is addressed to a person, if possible
- The cover letter discusses the position you are making an application for and where it was noted
- Your individual information is all included and accurate
- If you have a contact at the company, point out him or her in the very first paragraph of your cover letter
- The cover letter is targeted to the position you are making an application for
- The letter is focused, succinct, clear, and well-arranged
- If you have a gap in your work history, clarify it in your cover letter
- The font is simple to read
- No spelling or grammatical mistakes
- Read the cover letter aloud to ensure there are no missing words
- The cover letter is printed on high-quality bond paper matching your resume
- You have actually kept a copy for yourself
- Your letter is signed

When it concerns your resume, there are additionally a couple of things to remember. Much is the same when it comes to the cover letter, however you want your resume to be great too. Here's a list:

- There are no typographical or spelling mistakes
- The format is consistent throughout the whole file
- Utilize a high quality, heavier paper-- much heavier than regular copy paper
- You might wish to utilize a colored paper, however, make certain it is not garish like hot pink or neon green. Cream, gray, and off white are constantly excellent choices
- Utilize 8 ″" x 11" paper
- Print on only one side
- Utilize a font in between 10 and 14-- you want it to be simple to read and look pleasurable to the eye
- Utilize non-decorative fonts, however do not hesitate to experiment and utilize something a little interesting-- only not TOO interesting!
- Adhere to one font

- Stay away from italics, scripts, and highlighted words except for when highlighting your headings
- Do not utilize horizontal or vertical lines, graphics, or shading.
- Do not fold or staple your resume.
- If you need to mail your resume, put it in a big envelope and mail flat
- Make sure there is ample postage on the envelope to make it to the company
- When at all possible, provide your resume personally and ask to talk with the worker's director when you do so.
- Follow up after a reasonable time period if you have actually not heard anything. This reveals effort on your behalf and makes you unforgettable in the mind of the individual doing the hiring.

Chapter 7 - Sample Cover Letters

As we have actually claimed, the cover letter could be just as crucial as the resume, so you are going to want to have one that looks as professional and appealing as it can. These are a couple of sample letters that you might wish to utilize as a reference when crafting your own cover letters.

Example 1:

5 Apple Court

Eugene, OR 58367

305-666-4865

Mr. Gerald Weatherby

California Investments, Inc.

28 Sacramento Street

San Francisco, CA 40575

Dear Mr. Weatherby,

My outbound character, my sales experience, and my just recently finished education make me a strong prospect for a position as an insurance coverage broker for California Investments, Inc.

I just recently graduated from the University of Oregon with a degree in marketing, where I was president of both the Future Business Leaders of America and the American Marketing Association.

Although a recent graduate, I am not a common brand-new graduate. I went to school in Michigan, Arizona, and Oregon. And I have actually put myself through these schools by working such jobs as radio marketing sales, newspaper membership sales, and bartending, all of which improved my conventional education.

I have the maturity, abilities, and capabilities to start a profession in insurance coverage brokers, and I am looking to do this in California, my home state.

I am going to remain in California by the end of this month, and I'd like very much to talk with you about a position at California Investments. I am going to follow up this letter with a call to see if I can organize a time to meet with you.

Thank you for your time and consideration.

Sincerely,

Carl Oakley

Example 2:

19 Hickory Tree Way

Belle Mead, NJ 0582

(809) 333-3854

September 22, 2013

Ms. Kristin Keller

The Research Institute

43 Marketing Court

Princeton, NJ 04850

Dear Ms. Heller,

As marketing businesses are progressively called upon to supply information on magazine readership to publishers, there is a growing requirement for skilled and knowledgeable specialists in the field.

Through my marketing/research experiences and my master's thesis, which was focused on improving market research studies so they can much better specify magazine audiences to possible marketers, I am sure I might offer you valuable support in satisfying research study needs, handling crucial projects, and improving the marketing tools you presently utilize.

I am going to be finishing my master's degree in December and would be interested in making a substantial contribution to the Research Institute's success in a marketing/research capability.

I am certain my services would work for you, and I am going to call you in early October to discuss an interview.

Thank you for your time and consideration.

Sincerely,

Josh Harris

Example 3:

>9010 Peachtree Lane, # 3.
>
>Atlanta, GA 40404.
>
>505/666 -2020.

Ms. Joan Winters.

Atlanta Board of Education.

54 Peachtree Blvd

Atlanta, GA 20202.

Dear Ms. Winters,

I may be the "multi-talented teacher" you look for in your "Multi-Talented Teacher" ad in today's Atlanta Constitution. I'm a flexible teacher, all set to substitute, if needed, as early as next week. I have the strong teaching experience you define along with the strong computer abilities you want.

I am currently associated with an extremely regarded private primary school. Mr. Craig, the headmaster, is going to provide you an excellent reference. The details of your ad suggest to me that the position is going to include a number of the identical obligations that I am presently carrying out.

In addition to the preparation, administration, and student-parent counseling tasks I highlight in my resume, please note that I have a master's degree in addition to a teaching certificate from the state of Georgia.

Understanding how frenzied you need to be without a fifth-grade instructor, I am going to call you in a couple of days. Or, if you agree upon evaluating my letter and resume that I am the teacher you require, call me at the home number noted above, or at 444-8264 throughout business hours.

I am thanking you most sincerely for your time and consideration.

Cordially,

Anne Smith

These samples are more particular, however, maybe you would like some templates to work from for your particular situation.

Example 4:

Your Name

Your Address

Your City, State, Zip Code

Your Contact number

Your Email

Date

Name

Title

Company

Address

City, State, Postal Code

Dear Mr./ Ms. Last Name:

First Paragraph: The reason for your writing. Keep in mind to feature the name of a mutual contact, if you have one. Be clear and succinct concerning your request.

Middle Paragraphs: What you can offer. Encourage the readers that they need to approve the interview or appointment you asked for in the initial paragraph. Make connections between your capabilities and their requirements or your requirement for information and their capability to supply it. Keep in mind that you are translating your resume. Attempt to support each declaration you make with a piece of proof. Utilize a number of shorter paragraphs instead of one big block of text.

Last Paragraph: How you are going to follow up. Keep in mind that it is your obligation to follow-up; this relates to your job search. State that you are going to do so and offer the professional courtesy of suggesting when (one week's time is common). You might wish to decrease the time between sending your resume and follow up if you fax or e-mail it.

Sincerely,

Your Signature

Your Typed Name

Example 5:

Your Name

Your Address

Your City, State, Postal Code

Your Telephone number

Your Email

Date

Name

Title

Company

Address

City, State, Postal Code

Dear Mr./ Ms. Last Name:

Your Requirements:

- Responsible for evening operations in the Student Center and other centers, consisting of handling registration, resolving customer issues, handling risk management and emergencies, enforcement of department policies.
- Assists with hiring, training, and management of staff. Coordinates stats and inventory.
- Experience in the supervision of student personnel and strong social skills are additionally desired.
- Valid Minnesota driver's license with an excellent driving record. Capability to travel to various sites needed.
- Experience in collegiate programming and management.

My Qualifications:

- Register students for courses, design and handle program software, resolve customer issues, impose department policies, and act as a contact for students, faculty, and personnel.
- Hiring, training, scheduling, and management of personnel, handling supply inventory, and ordering what is needed.
- Minnesota driver's license with NTSA defensive driving accreditation.
- Comprehensive experience in collegiate programming and management.
- Exceptional social and communication abilities.

I value your putting in the time to evaluate my qualifications and experience. Once again, thank you for your consideration.

Sincerely,

Your Signature

Your Typed Name

Example 6:

Your name

Mailing address

City, state, and zip

Phone number(s).

Email address.

Today's date.

Your addressee's name.

Professional title.

Organization name.

Mailing address.

City, state and postal code

Dear Mr. (or Ms.) last name,

Begin your letter with a grabber-- a declaration that develops a connection with your reader, or a probing question. Quickly state what job you are making an application for.

The mid-section of your letter ought to be one or two brief paragraphs that make pertinent points about your certifications. You must not summarize your resume! You might add a column or bullet point format here.

Your last paragraph ought to initiate action by describing what you are going to do next (e.g., call the employer) or prompt the reader to call you to establish an interview. Close by stating, "thank you.".

Sincerely yours,

Your handwritten signature

Your name (typed).

Example 7:

Your Name.

Your Address.

Your City, State, Postal Code.

Your Contact number.

Your Email Address.

Date.

Company Contact Information.

Name.

Title.

Business.

Address.

City, State, Postal Code.

Salutation.

Dear Mr./ Ms.

Body of Cover Letter.

The body of your cover letter lets the company understand what position you are making an application for, why the employer ought to pick you for an interview, and how you are going to follow-up.

First Paragraph:

The very first paragraph of your letter ought to consist of information on why you are composing. Discuss the position you are making an application for. Include the name of a shared contact, if you have one. Be clear and succinct concerning your demand.

Middle Paragraphs:

The next part of your cover letter ought to explain what you need to provide the employer. Persuade the reader that they ought to grant the interview or appointment you asked for in the very first paragraph. Make strong connections between your capabilities and their requirements. Mention particularly how your abilities and experience match the job you are making an application for. Keep in mind that you are interpreting your resume, not duplicating it. Attempt to support each claim you make with proof. Utilize a number of briefer paragraphs or bullets instead of one big block of text.

Last Paragraph:

Wrap up your cover letter by thanking the employer for considering you for the position. Feature information on how you are going to follow-up. State that you are going to do so and specify when (one week's time is common). You might wish to decrease the time between sending your resume and follow up if you fax or e-mail it.

Complimentary Close:

Respectfully yours,

Signature:

Handwritten Signature (for a mailed letter).

Typed Signature.

Chapter 8 - Sample Reference Sheets.

Your reference sheet is necessary to have too-- as we pointed out previously. While this is not going to be sent by mail in addition to your resume and cover letter, you are going to still want to have it on hand throughout an interview so that you can produce it when your possible employer asks for it.

Here are some sample reference sheets for you when producing your own reference sheet.

Joan Smith.

PRESENT ADDRESS.

567 Hawkins Graduate Home.

West Lafayette, IN 46578

(643) 444-6735

PERMANENT ADDRESS

54367 N. College Avenue

Indianapolis, IN 4765

(645) 444-5887

REFERENCES

Professor Clark Dutch

Sociology Department

Purdue University

Stone Hall

West Lafayette, IN 9375

(985) 444-8345

Professor Dutch is my academic advisor and is currently supervising my research study in an independent research study sociology course.

Mrs. Sandra Sommer

Food Services Supervisor

Hawkins Graduate House

Purdue University

West Lafayette, IN 9375

(985) 465-4856

Mrs. Sommer was my supervisor when I worked in the Hawkins Cafeteria.

Mrs. Kate Morgan

Activity Therapy Personnel Wabash Valley Mental Health Center

1500 North River Road

West Lafayette, IN 9375

(985) 256-2853

Mrs. Morgan is my present employer.

References for Craig Wescott

475 Colby Hall

Hutchinson University

Hutchinson, IL 64783

(954-444-6578).

esterj01@hutch.edu.

Dr. John Wilson.

Professor of Psychology.

Hutchinson University.

Hutchinson, IL 64783.

wilsonj@hutch.edu.

(954-444-9475).

Dr. Wilson was my manager in the Human Subjects Research Laboratory.

Dr. Carl Mullins.

Professor of Biology.

Hutchinson University.

Hutchinson, IL 64783.

(954-444-8465).

Dr. Mullins was my professor in Biology 425: Special Research Projects.

Mr. Jack McMillen.

Project Director.

The Acme Corporation.

33452 Main Street.

Hutchinson, IL 64783.

(954-444-5869).

Mr. McMillen supervised my internship at the Acme Corporation.

Ms. Lauren Kirley.

Manager.

The Rasmussen Corporation.

2210 Elston Avenue.

Chicago, IL 54089.

(365-333-7594).

LKirley@rasmussen.com.

Ms. Kirley oversaw my co-op experience at the Rasmussen Corporation.

So you have your resume out there, and you got the telephone call for an interview. This next part is going to be quick, however, there are some things to remember when you are face to face with a potential employer throughout a job interview. Ideally, the advice from this book is going to aid you in getting the job!

Chapter 9 - The Interview.

The first thing that you wish to keep in mind when you are at a job interview is that first impressions count. Dress properly for the job. No matter what, however, never wear denim to a job interview-- it doesn't matter how casual the job is that you are making an application for, denim is improper in any such circumstance.

For ladies, a good skirt and dress or a suit are what you ought to wear. For guys, a suit is most proper, however, you can get away with a pair of khaki pants and a good polo shirt.

When you are speaking with your interviewer, be eager about the job. Communicate your enthusiasm about the opportunity of working for this organization, and don't forget to smile.

If you are making an application for a creative position or a teaching position, you may wish to bring along a portfolio of your work so that you can display your creativity. Having samples of what you can do can make you stand apart over other candidates.

Above all else, be delighted and passionate about your possible job. When you are delighted about being there, it is going to show in your disposition and your actions. I can't stress enough just how much this can make a distinction in getting the job and not getting the job.

Your job interview is when you get the opportunity to shine. Make sure to respond to all of the questions precisely and with excitement. Make an effort not to hesitate and be ready for anything. I once had an interview for a sales position where the job interviewer asked me to sell him a pen. I had the ability to think on my feet and offered him an excellent sales pitch. I got the job!

You could be just as effective when you put in the time to be ready for your interview. It is genuinely your character that is going to get you the job, together with your experience and your education.

When you get the interview, it is all up to you, however, you can do it. The individual interviewing you currently understands a lot about you from your wonderfully crafted resume that I have shown you how to create.

Conclusion

When you are searching for a job, having the right tools at hand is very essential. Those tools include having a killer resume in addition to an engaging cover letter that is going to assist potential companies with making the right choice by selecting you.

I have provided you with a great deal of advice about how to craft your resume to put your finest foot forward to make you look fantastic for the job and persuade them to call you first over any other candidate. What you want to do is stand apart over the competitors and make certain that you are the one that gets the interview!

There is a lot that enters into creating a resume that works. When you have all of the standard parts in place, you can make a resume that works for you and one that is going to assist you in getting a job. And, after all, that is your goal, isn't it?

Take your time making your resume and make sure that it shows who you are and what you can do. Let your resume speak for you and your capabilities and make sure to act on all of the places you have actually sent your resume to.

I hope that you have the ability to get your dream job with the guidance provided in this book. However, bear in mind that a great deal of the most fundamental parts have to do with you!

Best of luck and happy job searching!

I hope that you enjoyed reading through this book and that you have found it useful. If you want to share your thoughts on this book, you can do so by leaving a review on the Amazon page. Have a great rest of the day.

Manufactured by Amazon.ca
Bolton, ON